Skinny Scarves

LEISURE ARTS, INC. • Little Rock, Arkansas

SIMPLE RIB

Finished Size: 4" wide x 75" long
(10 cm x 190.5 cm)

SHOPPING LIST

Yarn (Medium Weight) 🧶 **MEDIUM 4**
[5 ounces, 266 yards
(140 grams, 243 meters) per
skein]:
☐ One skein
Knitting Needles
Straight needles,
☐ Size 8 (5 mm)
   or size needed for gauge

GAUGE INSTRUCTIONS

n pattern,
17 sts and 24 rows = 4" (10 cm)

INSTRUCTIONS

Cast on 17 sts.

Row 1 (Right side)**:** K1, (P1, K1) across.

Row 2: Purl across.

Repeat Rows 1 and 2 for pattern until
Scarf measures approximately
75" (190.5 cm) from cast on edge,
ending by working Row 2.

Bind off all sts in pattern.

BASKET WEAVE

 **EASY**

Finished Size: 4¼" wide x 75" long
(11 cm x 190.5 cm)

GAUGE INFORMATION

With larger size knitting needles,
in pattern, 20 sts = 4¼" (11 cm);
12 rows (one repeat) = 3¼"
(8.25 cm)

INSTRUCTIONS

With smaller size knitting needles,
cast on 20 sts.

Rows 1-5: Knit across.

Change to larger size knitting
needles.

Row 6: K3, purl across to last 3 sts, K3.

Row 7 (Right side)**:** K5, P4, K2, P4, K5.

Row 8: K3, P2, (K4, P2) twice, K3.

Rows 9 and 10: Repeat Rows 7 and 8.

Row 11: Knit across.

Row 12: K3, purl across to last 3 sts, K3.

Row 13: K3, P3, K2, P4, K2, P3, K3.

Row 14: K6, P2, K4, P2, K6.

Rows 15 and 16: Repeat Rows 13
and 14.

Row 17: Knit across.

Row 18: K3, purl across to last 3 sts, K3.

Repeat Rows 7-18 for pattern until
Scarf measures approximately
74¼" (188.5 cm) from cast on edge,
ending by working Row 10.

Change to smaller size knitting
needles.

Last 5 Rows: Knit across.

Bind off all sts in **knit**.

CELLULAR

Finished Size: 4" wide x 73½" long
(10 cm x 186.5 cm)

SHOPPING LIST

Yarn (Super Fine Weight) 🧶 **SUPER FINE 1**
[1.75 ounces, 166 yards
(50 grams, 152 meters) per skein]:
☐ 3 skeins

Knitting Needles
Straight needles,
☐ Size 6 (4 mm)
or size needed for gauge

GAUGE INFORMATION

In pattern, 24 sts = 4" (10 cm);
24 rows = 2½" (6.25 cm)

TECHNIQUES USED
- YO (*Fig. 1a, page 29*)
- K2 tog (*Fig. 2, page 30*)
- Slip 1 as if to **knit**, K2 tog, PSSO
  (*Fig. 4, page 30*)

INSTRUCTIONS
Cast on 24 sts.

Row 1: (K1, P1) across.

Row 2 (Right side)**:** (P1, K1) across.

Rows 3-5: Repeat Rows 1 and 2 once, then repeat Row 1 once **more**.

Row 6: (P1, K1) twice, ★ YO, slip 1 as if to **knit**, K2 tog, PSSO, YO, K1; repeat from ★ 3 times **more**, YO, K2, P1, K1: 25 sts.

Row 7: K1, P1, K1, purl across to last 2 sts, K1, P1.

Row 8: (P1, K1) twice, YO, K2 tog, YO, slip 1 as if to **knit**, K2 tog, PSSO, ★ YO, K1, YO, slip 1 as if to **knit**, K2 tog, PSSO; repeat from ★ 2 times **more**, K2, P1, K1: 24 sts.

Row 9: K1, P1, K1, purl across to last 2 sts, K1, P1.

Repeat Rows 6-9 for pattern until Scarf measures approximately 73" (185.5 cm) from cast on edge, ending by working Row 8.

Next Row: (K1, P1) across.

Next Row: (P1, K1) across.

Next Row: (K1, P1) across.

Last 2 Rows: Repeat last 2 rows.

Bind off all sts in pattern.

CLUSTER RIB

 **EASY**

Finished Size: 4¼" wide x 74" long
(11 cm x 188 cm)

GAUGE INFORMATION
With larger size knitting needles,
   in pattern,
   22 sts and 28 rows = 4¼" (10.75 cm)

TECHNIQUE USED
🎥 YO *(Fig. 1a, page 29)*

INSTRUCTIONS
With smaller size knitting needles,
cast on 22 sts.

Rows 1-4: Knit across.

Change to larger size knitting
needles.

Row 5 (Right side)**:** K3, P1, (K2, P1)
across to last 3 sts, K3.

Row 6: K4, YO, K2, with left needle
bring the YO over the 2 knit sts and
off the right needle, ★ K1, YO, K2,
with left needle bring the YO over
the 2 knit sts and off the right needle;
repeat from ★ 3 times **more**, K4.

Row 7: K3, P1, (K2, P1) across to last
3 sts, K3.

Repeat Rows 6 and 7 for pattern until
Scarf measures approximately 73¼"
(186 cm) from cast on edge, ending
by working Row 7.

Change to smaller size knitting
needles.

Last 4 Rows: Knit across.

Bind off all sts in **knit**.

EYELET GARTER

 **EASY**

Finished Size: 4" wide x 72¼" long
(10 cm x 183.5 cm)

SHOPPING LIST

Yarn (Medium Weight) **4**
[5 ounces, 230 yards
(141 grams, 211 meters) per skein]:
☐ 2 skeins

Knitting Needles

Straight needles,
☐ Size 8 (5 mm)
or size needed for gauge

GAUGE INFORMATION

In Garter Stitch,
18 sts and 32 rows = 4" (10 cm)

TECHNIQUES USED

YO (*Fig. 1a, page 29*)
K2 tog (*Fig. 2, page 30*)

INSTRUCTIONS

Cast on 18 sts.

Rows 1-3: Knit across.

Row 4: K3, (YO, K2 tog, K3) across.

Rows 5-7: Knit across.

Row 8: K5, YO, K2 tog, K3, YO, K2 tog, K6.

Repeat Rows 1-8 for pattern until Scarf measures approximately 72¼" (183.5 cm) from cast on edge, ending by working Row 3 **or** Row 7.

Bind off all sts in **knit**.

GARTER STRIPES

 **EASY**

Finished Size: 3¾" wide x 73½" long
(9.5 cm x 186.5 cm)

GAUGE INFORMATION

In Garter Stitch,
16 sts = 3¾" (9.5 cm);
14 rows = 1½" (3.75 cm)

INSTRUCTIONS

With Green, cast on 16 sts.

Row 1 (Right side)**:** Knit across.

Rows 2-12: Knit across.

Cut Green.

Rows 13-26: With Ecru, knit across.

Cut Ecru.

Rows 27-40: With Gold, knit across.

Cut Gold.

Rows 41-54: With Ecru, knit across.

Cut Ecru.

Rows 55-68: With Green, knit across.

Cut Green.

Repeat Rows 13-68 for pattern until Scarf measures approximately 73½" (186.5 cm) from cast on edge, ending by working Row 68.

Bind off all sts in **knit**.

MOCK CABLE

Finished Size: 4" wide x 73" long
(10 cm x 185.5 cm)

SHOPPING LIST

Yarn (Medium Weight) **4**
[3.5 ounces, 210 yards
(100 grams, 192 meters) per skein]:
☐ 2 skeins

Knitting Needles

Straight needles,
☐ Size 6 (4 mm) **and**
☐ Size 8 (5 mm)
or sizes needed for gauge

GAUGE INSTRUCTIONS

With larger size knitting needles,
in pattern, 23 sts (slightly stretched)
and 28 rows = 4" (10 cm)

TECHNIQUES USED

- YO (Fig. 1b, page 29)
- Slip 1 as if to **knit**, K2, PSSO2
(Figs. 3a & b, page 30)

INSTRUCTIONS

With smaller size knitting needles,
cast on 23 sts.

Rows 1-4: Knit across.

Change to larger size knitting
needles.

Row 5 (Right side)**:** K3, P2, ★ slip 1 as
if to **knit**, K2, PSSO2, P2; repeat from
★ 2 times **more**, K3: 20 sts.

Row 6: K5, P1, YO, P1, (K2, P1, YO, P1)
twice, K5: 23 sts.

Row 7: K3, (P2, K3) across.

Row 8: K5, P3, (K2, P3) twice, K5.

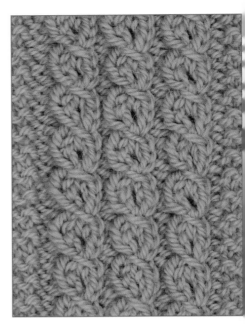

Row 9: K3, P2, ★ slip 1 as if to **knit**,
K2, PSSO2, P2; repeat from ★ 2 times
more, K3: 20 sts.

Repeat Rows 6-9 for pattern until
Scarf measures approximately
72¼" (183.5 cm) from cast on edge,
ending by working Row 7.

Change to smaller size knitting
needles.

Last 4 Rows: Knit across.

Bind off all sts in **knit**.

RUFFLED

 **EASY**

Finished Size: 4" wide x 62" long
(10 cm x 157.5 cm)

SHOPPING LIST

Yarn
(Mesh Super Bulky Weight)

This is a novelty mesh yarn that is used for ruffle scarves.

[3.5 ounces, 30 yards
(100 grams, 27 meters) per ball]:

☐ One ball

If you want your Scarf to be longer, buy 2 balls of yarn.

Knitting Needles

Straight needles,

☐ Size 9 (5.5 mm)
  or size needed for gauge

Additional Supplies

☐ Sewing needle
☐ Matching thread
☐ Point protectors (optional)

GAUGE INSTRUCTIONS

Gauge is not important.

TIP: To keep the stitches from slipping off the needle when you lay your work down, we suggest placing a point protector on the needle.

INSTRUCTIONS

📹 It's the unique texture of mesh yarn that creates fullness in these beautiful ruffles. Let us show you how to get the best results with mesh yarn — we made a video just for you at www.LeisureArts.com/5948.

Stretch yarn out so you can see all the mesh, having the mesh edge at the top and the solid edge at the bottom. You will knit with the loops at the top edge (*Fig. A*).

Fig. A

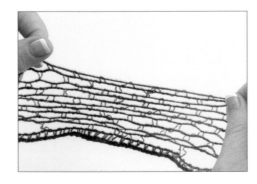

Row 1: Beginning 4" (10 cm) from the end and working from **left** to **right**, insert the needle from **back** to **front** through one loop (*Fig. B*), ★ skip the next loop, insert the needle from **back** to **front** in the next loop (*Fig. C*); repeat from ★ 4 times **more**: 6 sts.

Now that the stitches are on the needle, you are ready to start knitting from right to left.

Fig. B

Fig. C

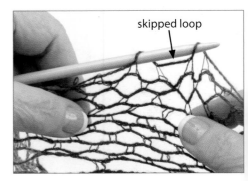

skipped loop

Row 2: Insert right needle in first st. Skip the next loop *(Fig. D)*, pick up the next loop to the right, place it on the right needle and knit the st *(Fig. E)*, ★ skip the next loop, using the next loop, knit the next st; repeat from ★ across.

Fig. D

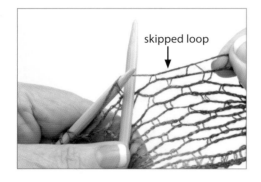

skipped loop

Repeat Row 2 until Scarf measures approximately 62" (157.5 cm) from beginning edge, leaving a 12" (30.5 cm) length for binding off.

Bind off all sts in **knit** *(Fig. F)*.

Fig. F

Using sewing needle and matching thread, sew the last loop in place *(Fig. G)*; do **not** cut thread. Tuck remaining end under last ruffle and with same thread, sew in place *(Fig. H)*.

Fig. G

Fig. H

Tuck the beginning end under the first ruffle. Using sewing needle and thread, sew in place.

SEED STITCH

 EASY

Finished Size: 3¼" wide x 72" long
(8.25 cm x 183 cm)

SHOPPING LIST

Yarn (Bulky Weight) **⑤**

[3 ounces, 144 yards
(85 grams, 132 meters) per skein**]:**

☐ One skein

Knitting Needles

Straight needles,

☐ Size 10 (6 mm)

or size needed for gauge

GAUGE INSTRUCTIONS

In Seed Stitch,

11 sts and 24 rows = 3¼"
(8.25 cm)

INSTRUCTIONS

Cast on 11 sts.

Row 1: K1, (P1, K1) across.

Repeat Row 1 for Seed Stitch until
Scarf measures approximately
72" (183 cm) from cast on edge.

Bind off all sts in pattern.

SIMPLE CABLE

 **EASY**

Finished Size: 3¼" wide x 74¾" long
(8.25 cm x 190 cm)

SHOPPING LIST

Yarn (Medium Weight) **4 MEDIUM**
[3.5 ounces, 200 yards
(100 grams, 182 meters) per skein]:
☐ 2 skeins

Knitting Needles
Straight needles,
☐ Size 6 (4 cm) **and**
☐ Size 8 (5 mm)
or sizes needed for gauge

Additional Supplies
☐ Cable needle

GAUGE INSTRUCTIONS
With larger size knitting needles,
in pattern,
18 sts and 24 rows = 3¼" (8.25 cm)

——— STITCH GUIDE ———
FRONT CABLE (uses next 6 sts)
Slip next 3 sts onto cable needle
and hold in **front** of work, K3 from
left needle, K3 from cable needle.

INSTRUCTIONS
With smaller size knitting needles,
cast on 18 sts.

Rows 1-4: Knit across.

Change to larger size knitting
needles.

Row 5 (Right side)**:** K3, P3, K6, P3, K3.

Row 6: K6, P6, K6.

Rows 7 and 8: Repeat Rows 5 and 6.

Row 9: K3, P3, work Front Cable,
P3, K3.

Row 10: K6, P6, K6.

Row 11: K3, P3, K6, P3, K3.

Row 12: K6, P6, K6.

Rows 13-16: Repeat Rows 11
and 12 twice.

Repeat Rows 9-16 for pattern until
Scarf measures approximately
74" (188 cm) from cast on edge,
ending by working Row 14.

Change to smaller size knitting
needles.

Last 4 Rows: Knit across.

Bind off all sts in **knit**.

CROCUS BUDS

Finished Size: 4" wide x 75" long
   (10 cm x 190.5 cm)

SHOPPING LIST

Yarn (Medium Weight) **4**
[1.75 ounces, 147 yards
(50 grams, 135 meters) per skein]:

☐ 2 skeins

Knitting Needles

Straight needles,

☐ Size 8 (5 mm)
   or size needed for gauge

GAUGE INSTRUCTIONS

In pattern,
   17 sts and 24 rows = 4" (10 cm)

TECHNIQUE USED

YO *(Fig. 1a, page 29)*

INSTRUCTIONS

Cast on 17 sts.

Rows 1-4: Knit across.

Row 5 (Right side)**:** K4, YO, (K2, YO) across to last 5 sts, K5: 22 sts.

Row 6: K3, P1, ★ P3, with left needle bring the third st on right needle over the first 2 sts and off the needle; repeat from ★ across to last 3 sts, K3: 17 sts.

Row 7: K5, YO, (K2, YO) across to last 4 sts, K4: 22 sts.

Row 8: K3, ★ P3, with left needle, bring the third st on right needle over the first 2 sts and off the needle; repeat from ★ across to last 4 sts, P1, K3: 17 sts.

Repeat Rows 5-8 for pattern until Scarf measures approximately 74½" (189 cm) from cast on edge, ending by working Row 6 **or** Row 8.

Last 5 Rows: Knit across.

Bind off all sts in **knit**.

DIAMONDS

Finished Size: 4" wide x 73½" long
(10 cm x 186.5 cm)

SHOPPING LIST

Yarn (Light Weight)
[2.2 ounces, 102 yards
(65 grams, 93 meters) per ball]:
☐ 3 balls

Knitting Needles

Straight needles,
☐   Size 6 (4 mm)
   or size needed for gauge

GAUGE INSTRUCTIONS

In pattern, 24 sts = 4" (10 cm);
   24 rows = 2½" (6.25 cm)

STITCH GUIDE

 LEFT TWIST *(abbreviated LT)*
(uses 2 sts)

Working **behind** first stitch on left
needle, purl into the back of second
stitch *(Fig. A)* making sure **not** to drop
stitches off, then knit the first stitch
(Fig. B) letting both stitches drop off
the needle.

Fig. A

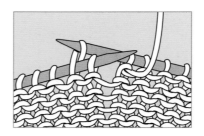

Fig. B

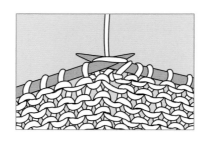

RIGHT TWIST *(abbreviated RT)*
(uses 2 sts)

Knit second stitch on left needle
(Fig. C) making sure **not** to drop
stitches off, then purl the first stitch
(Fig. D) letting both stitches drop
off needle.

Fig. C

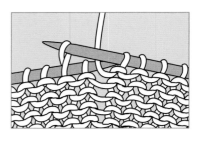

Fig. D

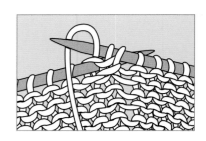

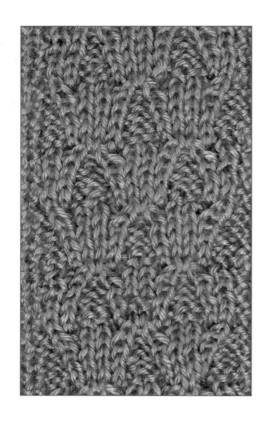

INSTRUCTIONS

Cast on 24 sts.

Row 1: (K1, P1) across.

Row 2 (Right side)**:** (P1, K1) across.

Rows 3 and 4: Repeat Rows 1 and 2.

Row 5: K1, P1, K2, P1, K2, (P2, K2) 3 times, P1, (K1, P1) twice.

Row 6: P1, K1, P2, K1, P1, RT, LT, P1, K2, P1, RT, LT, (P1, K1) 3 times.

Row 7: (K1, P1, K2, P1) twice, K1, P2, K1, P1, K2, P1, (K1, P1) 3 times.

Row 8: P1, K1, P2, K1, RT, P2, LT, K2, RT, P2, LT, K1, (P1, K1) twice.

Row 9: K1, P1, K2, P2, K4, P4, K4, P2, (K1, P1) twice.

Row 10: P1, K1, P1, knit across to last 2 sts, P1, K1.

Row 11: K1, P1, K2, P1, K2, (P2, K2) 3 times, P1, K3, P1.

Row 12: P1, K1, P2, (LT, P1, K2, P1, RT) twice, P3, K1.

Row 13: K1, P1, K3, P1, K1, (P2, K1, P1, K2, P1, K1) twice, P1.

Row 14: P1, K1, P3, (LT, K2, RT, P2) twice, K1, P1, K1.

Row 15: K1, P1, (K4, P4) twice, K3, P1, K1, P1.

Row 16: P1, K1, P1, knit across to last 2 sts, P1, K1.

Repeat Rows 5-16 for pattern until Scarf measures approximately 73" (185.5 cm) from cast on edge, ending by working Row 16.

Next Row: (K1, P1) across.

Next Row: (P1, K1) across.

Last 2 Rows: Repeat last 2 rows.

Bind off all sts in pattern.

ABBREVIATIONS

cm	centimeters
K	knit
LT	Left Twist
mm	millimeters
P	purl
PSSO	pass slipped stitch over
PSSO2	pass slipped stitch over 2 sts
RT	Right Twist
st(s)	stitch(es)
tog	together
YO	yarn over

SYMBOLS & TERMS

★ — work instructions following ★ as many **more** times as indicated in addition to the first time.

( ) or [ ] — work enclosed instructions **as many** times as specified by the number immediately following **or** contains explanatory remarks.

colon (:) — the number(s) given after a colon at the end of a row denote(s) the number of stitches you should have on that row.

GAUGE

Exact gauge is **essential** for proper size. Before beginning your Scarf, make a sample swatch using the yarn and needles specified in the individual instructions. After completing the swatch, measure it, counting your stitches and rows carefully. If your swatch is larger or smaller than specified, **make another, changing needle size to get the correct gauge.** Keep trying until you find the size needles that will give you the specified gauge.

Yarn Weight Symbol & Names	LACE 0	SUPER FINE 1	FINE 2	LIGHT 3	MEDIUM 4	BULKY 5	SUPER BULKY 6
Type of Yarns in Category	Fingering, size 10 crochet thread	Sock, Fingering, Baby	Sport, Baby	DK, Light Worsted	Worsted, Afghan, Aran	Chunky, Craft, Rug	Bulky, Roving
Knit Gauge Range* in Stockinette St to 4" (10 cm)	33-40** sts	27-32 sts	23-26 sts	21-24 sts	16-20 sts	12-15 sts	6-11 sts
Advised Needle Size Range	000-1	1 to 3	3 to 5	5 to 7	7 to 9	9 to 11	11 and larger

*GUIDELINES ONLY: The chart above reflects the most commonly used gauges and needle sizes for specific yarn categories.

** Lace weight yarns are usually knitted on larger needles to create lacy openwork patterns. Accordingly, a gauge range is difficult to determine. Always follow the gauge stated in your pattern.

KNITTING NEEDLES																		
U.S.	0	1	2	3	4	5	6	7	8	9	10	10½	11	13	15	17	19	35	50
U.K.	13	12	11	10	9	8	7	6	5	4	3	2	1	00	000	---	---	---	---
Metric - mm	2	2.25	2.75	3.25	3.5	3.75	4	4.5	5	5.5	6	6.5	8	9	10	12.75	15	19	25

YARN OVERS

A yarn over *(abbreviated YO)* is simply placing the yarn over the right needle creating an extra stitch. Since the yarn over produces a hole in the knit fabric, it is used for a lacy effect. On the row following a yarn over, you must be careful to keep it on the needle and treat it as a stitch by knitting or purling it as instructed.

To make a yarn over, you'll loop the yarn over the needle like you would to knit or purl a stitch, bringing it either to the front or to the back of the piece so that it'll be ready to work the next stitch, creating a new stitch on the needle.

After a knit stitch, before a knit stitch

Bring the yarn forward **between** the needles, then back **over** the top of the right-hand needle, so that it is now in position to **knit** the next stitch *(Fig. 1a)*.

After a purl stitch, before a purl stitch

Take the yarn **over** the right-hand needle to the back, then forward **under** it, so that it is now in position to **purl** the next stitch *(Fig. 1b)*.

Fig. 1a

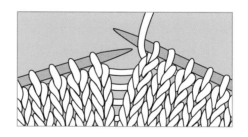

Fig. 1b

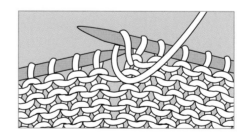

KNIT TERMINOLOGY	
UNITED STATES	INTERNATIONAL
gauge =	tension
bind off =	cast off
yarn over (YO) =	yarn forward (yfwd) **or** yarn around needle (yrn)

◕☐☐☐ BEGINNER	Projects for first-time knitters using basic knit and purl stitches. Minimal shaping.
◕■☐☐ EASY	Projects using basic stitches, repetitive stitch patterns, simple color changes, and simple shaping and finishing.
◕■■☐ INTERMEDIATE	Projects with a variety of stitches, such as basic cables and lace, simple intarsia, double-pointed needles and knitting in the round needle techniques, mid-level shaping and finishing.
◕■■■ EXPERIENCED	Projects using advanced techniques and stitches, such as short rows, fair isle, more intricate intarsia, cables, lace patterns, and numerous color changes.

KNIT 2 TOGETHER (abbreviated K2 tog)

Insert the right needle into the **front** of the first two stitches on the left needle as if to **knit** (Fig. 2), then **knit** them together as if they were one stitch.

Fig. 2

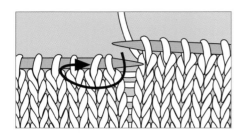

SLIP 1, KNIT 2, PASS SLIPPED STITCH OVER 2 STITCHES (abbreviated slip 1, K2, PSSO2)

Slip one stitch as if to **knit** (Fig. 3a). Knit the next two stitches. With the left needle, bring the slipped stitch over the two stitches just made (Fig. 3b) and off the needle.

Fig. 3a

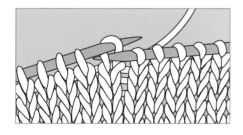

Fig. 3b

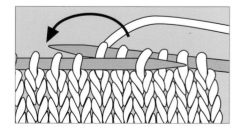

SLIP 1, KNIT 2 TOGETHER, PASS SLIPPED STITCH OVER

(abbreviated slip 1, K1, PSSO)

Slip one stitch as if to **knit** (Fig. 3a). Knit the next two stitches together (Fig. 2). With the left needle, bring the slipped stitch over the stitch just made (Fig. 4) and off the needle.

Fig. 4

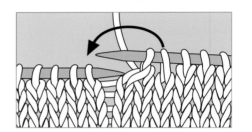

YARN INFORMATION

The Scarves in this leaflet were made using various weights of yarn. Any brand of the weight specified may be used. It is best to refer to the yardage/meters when determining how many balls or skeins to purchase. Remember, to arrive at the finished size, it is the GAUGE/TENSION that is important, not the brand of yarn.

For your convenience, listed below are the specific yarns used to create our photography models.

SIMPLE RIB
Red Heart® Super Tweed™
#7819 Landshark

BASKET WEAVE
Caron® Simply Soft®
#0014 Pagoda

CELLULAR
Patons® Kroy Socks FX
#57510 Copper Colors

CLUSTER RIB
Caron® Simply Soft®
#9703 Bone

EYELET GARTER
Red Heart® With Love™
#1816 Waterlily

GARTER STRIPES
Lion Brand® Wool-Ease®
Ecru - #099 Fisherman
Gold - #171 Gold
Green - #172 Lemongrass

MOCK CABLE
Patons® Classic Wool
#77201 Aquarium

RUFFLED
Red Heart® Boutique™ Sashay™
#1943 Tango

SEED STITCH
Lion Brand® Tweed Stripes®
#206 Woodlands

SIMPLE CABLE
Bernat® Satin
#04531 Rouge

CROCUS BUDS
Lion Brand® Amazing®
#201 Ruby

DIAMONDS
Patons® Silk Bamboo
#85046 Stone

Your opinion matters!

WE WOULD LOVE TO HEAR if our online video instructions and the new format of our publications are helpful to you!

PLEASE SHARE your comments and suggestions at
www.facebook.com/Official.LeisureArts

At Leisure Arts, we're excited about bringing you the most complete, easy-to-follow instructions. Let us know how we can make your creative experiences more fun, more rewarding--and yes, even easier!

Production Team: Writer/Technical Editor - Lois J. Long; Editorial Writer - Susan McManus Johnson; Senior Graphic Artist - Lora Puls; Graphic Artists - Jessica Bramlett and Becca Snider Tally; Photo Stylist - Brooke Duszota; and Photographer - Jason Masters.